SHTF Prepping

100+ Amazing Tips, Tricks, Hacks & DIY Prepper Projects, Along With 77 Items You Need In Your STHF Stockpile Now! (Off Grid Living, SHTF Arsenal, Urban Prepping & Disaster Preparedness Survival Guide)

Kevin Moore © 2015

Disclaimer:

Introduction

First off, I'd like to thank you for purchasing my book. This book will give you a good idea of what you need to do in order to properly prepare for an SHTF situation. I'll go over everything from creating a bug out bag, to showing you how to live off the grid, and survive long term after a disaster. After reading this book, you'll have a good foundation of what you'll need to do in order to keep yourself and your family safe should you be thrown into an emergency situation.

The world we live in can get crazy at times. New threats always seem to be looming on the horizon. One second, everything is perfect, and the next second disaster strikes and turns everything upside down. This type of situation happens all over the world every day. Natural disasters, medical outbreaks, and civil war, uproot millions of innocent people's lives each year. Just because it hasn't happened to you yet doesn't mean it won't happen in the future. Who knows what might happen going forward. That's why I believe in being prepared. SHTF prepping is a vital part of any good disaster preparedness plan.

I was taught to wish for the best but always prepare for the worst. I've lived by those words for most of my adult life and they haven't failed me yet. Hopefully, I can instill some of the things I've learned along the way to help you get ready for any SHTF situation.

Everyone in the world needs at least three things to survive. These three things are food, water, and shelter. If you don't have a reliable source for all three, your odds of surviving will be reduced drastically. In this book, I'll go over all three of these areas, and show you what steps you need to start taking in advance to be properly prepared. Building an SHTF stockpile, learning new survival skills, and getting all your other preps and projects in place will take time, hard work and some money. The longer you give yourself to accomplish the tasks at hand, the higher chance you'll have of successfully accomplishing everything you've set forth to do.

Let's get started!

Chapter One An Introduction to SHTF Prepping

Creating an SHTF Survival Disaster Preparedness Plan

Knowing your long term plans and strategy, in the event of a disaster is one of the most critical aspects of successfully surviving long-term. If you don't have a plan in place, or your plan is incomplete and missing important components, you might not recover from it. In this section, I'll discuss some of the most important questions you'll need to ask yourself and have answered before getting started.

- Where will you and your family take shelter?

- Do you have a backup shelter plan in place in case something happens to your main shelter?

- Is your shelter close to a legitimate water source that you can easily access?

- Is your shelter warm, dry, and able to be secured from attackers?

- Do you have access to both food and shelter in the same location, or are they separate from one another.

- How many people will you have in your group?

- Do you have a plan in place to keep your food secure and dry?

- Will you have different stockpiles in multiple locations?

- How long can your stockpile last?

- What is your plan for replenishing your stockpile, and any other tools, or weapons you need to survive long term?

- Do you have a comprehensive first aid kit?

- How will you keep your family or group safe from an attacker?

- Do you have any weapons training or medical training? If not, do you plan on getting any?

As you may have noticed there's a lot of things you'll need to think about before creating an SHTF disaster preparedness survival plan. Only after you've worked out the answers to these important questions can you really begin to get a plan put into place.

I like to think of my plan being divided into three different main stages. The fist stage is my short term plans (months 1-4). The second stage is my mid-term plans (5 months – 1 year). The final stage is my long term plan (1 year+). Each of these stages should be thoroughly thought out and prepared for. If you fail to do this, you could end up prepping incorrectly, or end up wasting preps you spent time on, due to poor planning.

Remember, stockpiling your rations is the easiest part of the process. The harder parts involve knowing how long your preps will last, how you're going to use them, and what you're plans are when you're stockpile runs low.

I suggest keeping detailed records of all of your preps and every item in your stockpile. It's important to know the quantity of each item when you added the item to your stockpile, the expiration date of your food, any instructions needed on how to operate something you've purchased, and a schedule for rotating your food so you're always eating things before they spoil and go to waste.

The better you keep these records and the more time you spend organizing your stockpile, the better your chances of surviving long term. This may all feel a bit daunting at first, but I assure you these are rather simple habits to form once you get going. The sooner you get started the better. Within no time, these habits will become second nature and a part of your daily routine.

Please do not keep your prepping records online. When an emergency occurs, you'll likely lose the Internet and possibly your power if you don't have some kind of generator. If you don't have a way to access all your records, then your work planning and cataloging everything will have been done in vain. In an emergency situation, knowledge is a powerful advantage. The more you have the better off you'll be.

I suggest once you've mapped out your plan, you then come up with a secondary one in case the first plan is comprised. You'll want to have escape routes and alternate locations picked out in advance in case something drives you from your base of operations. I would have some bug out locations scouted, and I would hide some supplies along your escape routes that you can reach if needed.

Having contingencies are an important part of any disaster preparedness plan. Things rarely work out exactly as we envision they will. Giving yourself multiple options will only improve your chances. Personally, I have multiple strategies and plans mapped out for each kind of major disaster. This way I have a plan that is specifically tailored to whatever type of SHTF situation my family and I find ourselves in. I also keep stockpiles in a three other bug out locations, should certain areas become dangerous and unsafe.

Finally, and the importance of this can't be stressed enough CONSTANTLY BE DRILLING! You can make plans till your face turns blue, but if you can't execute those plans properly, then you were just wasting your time. When I began running drills, I was shocked at the amount of things we missed in the planning stages. Not only that, but we had trouble executing our plans correctly in a timely fashion. Remember, in an emergency situation things will only be more difficult as you'll have to deal with higher levels of stress and fear. It took some time but now when my family drills we're a well-oiled unit. Since I live primarily on the road with my family RVing around the country we need to drill more often, because there's a lot more variables involved depending on our location at the time.

Remember, when a disaster occurs you need to know you're initial plans inside and out. You want to be able to react off of instinct, and not have to think too long on what you're next steps will be. I suggest drilling at least once a month, at different times of the day, and always focus on tweaking or improving any areas you think need it.

The Basics Behind SHTF Prepping

The Preppers Checklist

1. Create a binder for all your important papers and documents. This is a very important resource to have handy. It's good not only for big emergencies but also smaller emergencies that might come up in your everyday lives. Some of the items you should include in your binder are birth certificates, social security cards, divorce & marriage documents, passports, insurance and mortgage papers, medical records, diplomas, prescription lists and immunization records. You'll want to keep this binder somewhere safe but accessible. I have my binder stored safely in a small fireproof box located in an easy to reach hidden safe.

2. Make a list of skills you'll want to start learning. Then take your list and place all the skills in the order of most importance to least importance. That way you can begin learning new skills based on their priority level. Some skills to consider adding to your list include self-defense, weapons training, first aid, cooking, gardening, and hunting.

3. Create a food and supplies journal. Use these journals to document everything you and your family consume during the course of one week. This should be an extremely thorough accounting, so please don't skip over things or leave out stuff because you don't think it's important enough for inclusion. Having an accurate assessment will go a long way in giving you an idea on how to craft the ideal list for your long term supplies and food storage.

4. Create a detailed survival plan and a safety plan on how you'll defend your homestead from possible intrusion. You'll want to know what measures you'll have in place to deter attackers and what weapons, ammunition and gear you'll need in order to properly defend your property. You should also have escape routes planned and alternate locations to fall back to in case needed.

5. Do a full inspection of all your vehicles and a top to bottom inspection of your home. You need to go over every inch of both your vehicles and home to find and fix any issues you come across. You want to begin getting all the issues fixed now before disaster strikes and make fixing things much more difficult. You also want to make sure your vehicles are in top shape, in case you ever need to bug out of your residence quickly. The last thing you want is a breakdown during an emergency situation.

6. Depending on your living situation and space you're working with, I would suggest you begin cutting and storing firewood. Having enough wood to use as fuel will be very important in an SHTF situation. This is especially true if a disaster occurs during the colder winter months when the need for additional heat is at a premium.

7. Prepare bug out bags for both you and any family members. Everyone should have their own bag, and know exactly what's inside them. These bags need to be ready in advance, so if you're forced to leave at a moment's notice you'll still be prepared.

8. Begin a fitness routine. Off grid living requires a lot of hard work and determination. The better shape you're in physically the better you'll be able to meet the new demands you'll be forced to deal with in order to survive. I enjoy hiking and climbing. It not only helps me stay fit but I'm also learning a lot of different skills by being out in nature at the same time.

9. Begin your stockpile. Besides food, you need to stock up on fuel, household supplies, tools, weapons, batteries and a variety of other things I'll touch on later in this book. I suggest you also stock up on things to keep you and your family entertained during down time. This includes things like games and books. I'd also recommend starting a collection of DIY, how to, medical, and cookbooks. If something goes wrong once SHTF, you won't be able to call someone else for help. Instead, it will be up to you to figure out a solution to the problem. Having these books on hand can be a real lifesaver.

10. Create a dental kit and first aid kit. These should be as comprehensive as you can possibly make them. If things go south, you'll find that getting medicine or medical services will become extremely difficult if not impossible. I also suggest getting some basic medical training on how to treat minor injuries, wounds and burns. I would also take a course in CPR training.

Chapter Two: Food & Water Long Term Survival Guide

Growing & Raising Your Own Food

Many people often assume our country has the most abundant and safest food supply in the world. They feel our food supply can offer the most choices and convenience while also offering the lowest costs. While some of this may be true, in an SHTF situation our food supply would run out alarmingly fast.

I believe, like many others, that food we've grown ourselves, or sourced from local farms is almost always better in taste and nutritional value than anything we can purchase from a store. Now I understand everyone won't have the land needed to raise their own animals and grow massive gardens. However, if you're creative, you can grow a good amount of food from just a small herb and vegetable garden. The point is to start learning how to provide your own food while prepping in order to make you better prepared in case of a disaster.

Another great reason for starting early and growing your food now is how much savings it can provide to help fund your other preps. Once you get your garden set up and producing food, you'll be able to slash your food bill down to next to nothing. This will allow you to stock up on everything you'll need in case of an emergency. This will also allow you to begin creating your long term food storage plan. Now, if something bad does happen, you'll have more food already stored. You won't need to wait for more food to grow as you start your garden because it will already be up and producing your food. Don't get me wrong, growing food requires patience and hard work, but the benefits of extra food security definitely outweigh the negatives.

Back in the era of the Great Depression, there were millions of people who felt a real sense of hunger. These people had lost all their savings and were no longer able to provide food for their families. The saving grace for people back then was that most people already knew how to garden and grow their own sources of food. This meant they had the ability to supplement dwindling food stores with the food they were growing themselves and then barter with their neighbors for everything else they needed.

Fast forward to our modern day and age. How many people now do you think would be able to grow their own food, if the world faced a similar situation. Unfortunately, not nearly as many. People have grown lazier and less educated in the ways of farming due to all the modern conveniences invented over the last 70 years.

Knowing the kind of food you want to begin growing is a crucial part of any serious prepper's life. You need to do your planning far in advance so you can implement it effectively and pivot to other options if a change is needed.

Another thing you'll need to decide on is your preferred gardening techniques. There are many different methods employed when growing food. I suggest reading up on a few and choosing the one that speaks to you. For example, I've employed a bio-intensive gardening technique in the past. This form of gardening focuses on 8 principles that let me produce higher yields than a less intensive approach might.

The 8 Principles of Bio-Intensive Gardening:

1. Composting

2. Intensive Planting

3. Deep Soil Preparation

4. Companion Planting

5. Growing Crops for Carbons and Grains

6. Using Open Pollinated Seeds

7. Growing High-Calorie Crops in Small Areas

8. Integrating All These Processes Into an Interrelated System

Using this type of bio-intensive gardening, my garden beds are all always double dug, and any compost used has been made from crops that were specifically used to serve that particular purpose. Some of those crops, like corn, for instance, can also provide us with some food. Using all these techniques together, one can create a balanced system, which not only helps to serve the purpose of feeding the soil but also ends up improving and building up the entire ecosystem.

Whatever techniques you decide on using, always be sure to keep thorough records and plan out well in advance the amount of food you need to grow. Having precisely detailed records will better inform you on how to improve your gardening process in the years to come. You'll be able to look back and see precisely what things worked and what didn't. You'll also be able to see what types of foods you grew too much of, and what types of food you need to start planting more of going forward.

In order to truly rely on your garden, in terms of properly feeding your loved ones, you'll need to grow some staple crops. These are the types of food that form the foundation of a human diet. To build a system of self-sufficiency, your crops need to be both easy to harvest and to store, they also need to return a strong yield, and they need to be foods that are dense in calories.

Types Of Food to Grow

In this section, I'll discuss some of the kinds of food you'll want to think of growing when preparing for an SHTF situation.

Sweet Potatoes & Potatoes - These are an amazing source of calories, that can be prepared in a variety of different ways. These are also extremely easy to both grow and keep safely stored. Potatoes take between 65 and 90 days to harvest depending on the kind of variety you happen to be using.

Grain Corn – These come in many different varieties, with some being more suited to certain types of climates than others. I would research which kind grow well in your location. Grain corn can be ground up into cornmeal and then from that made into a lot of different foods, everything from polenta and pudding, to pancakes and bread.

Wheat – Growing this type of food will allow you to make plenty of bread to help feed your family throughout the entire year, with enough still left over to barter or trade with.

Dry Beans – There are almost a countless variety of different beans you can grow. Much like grain corn, some will fare better in certain kinds of climates. Beans are a wonderful staple food as they are both rich in flavor and dense in needed calories. There also easy to store for long periods of time which make them great for preppers.

Vegetable Gardens & Herb Gardens – I would suggest every prepper at least have a herb & vegetable garden. I can't stress enough how important gardening is in any long-term survival plan. Even if you don't have a lot of room start small and start developing your skills on a small herb or vegetable garden. In my garden, I also try and grow as much fruit as I can. I grew peppers, tomatoes, carrots, cabbage, cucumbers, celery and kale among other foods. Feel free to add in a few of your favorites or subtract the ones you're not crazy about.

Top Animals to Consider Owning for Food

Before I started splitting my time between the road and my homestead, I used to raise a few different animals (primarily chickens and goats). Having a few animals can be a great source of food, milk and wool. If you're planning to live off the grid, or just want to be better prepared for an emergency scenario than here is a list of animals you might consider owning and why.

Remember, if you ever get an animal that's more than you can handle you can always sell the animal to someone else who needs it. Once I decided not to live at my home full time, I sold off all my livestock to a neighbor of mine.

Chickens (Meat & Eggs) – These animals are my personal favorite. They can provide you with fresh eggs daily, and are a wonderful source of meat. These animals are also very simple to maintain. If you decide to raise chickens for meat I do suggest investing in a mechanical chicken plucker. It will save you a ton of time and energy.

Ducks (Meat & Eggs) – They are a great source of meat and also lay big eggs. These animals are also quiet and easy to maintain.

Goats (Cheese, Meat & Milk) – These are great animals, that are friendly, but can be difficult to keep fenced in properly at times. Not only do they provide milk and cheese, but there a good source of meat and can even be helpful in clearing any overgrown land on your property.

Rabbits (Meat) – These are a good source of meat and they are much easier to process than chickens.

Dairy Cow (Milk) – Great source of both cream and milk.

Beef Cattle (Meat) – One can provide enough meat to fill up your freezer for a winter.

Sheep (Meat, Milk & Wool) – Friendly animals that provide milk and wool. Also a good source of meat.

Remember, owning and properly caring for livestock is a very big commitment. I would start off small and see what animals might work best for your specific situation. Do some research before actually procuring any animals. The last thing you want to do is accidentally kill your animals through improper care. It's not only cruel and wasteful, but it will cost you your investment in the animal, and everything they'd provide you going forward.

A Guide to Long Term Food Storage

Having a solid well thought out plan in place for your long term food storage and water storage is a key element of any prepper household. When you're relying on only yourself, you need to ensure you'll have the supplies needed to survive. If you've forgotten something you're out of luck. In a disaster situation, you just can't go to a local store and pick up what you need.

In my home, I have a very large dry basement that I've since converted into a fully stocked food and water storage area. I designed and built a large number of shelving units for all my food along with a large water storage system for holding over 300 gallons of water. Doing all this in advance gave me good peace of mind and assured I was prepared for whatever might happen. With all my systems and preps in place, I'm able to easily keep a good track of my food and water, making any adjustments on the fly as I deem necessary. Be sure the area you use is dry and cool. You don't want your food to get wet, too hot or too cold.

When deciding on what to store long term, you first need to know what items can be stored for long periods of time, exactly how long they can be stored for, and how you plan on using or rotating out food before it expires. I would also recommend learning to can and preserve your own food. You will also want to learn how to properly cure meat.

Down below is a bunch of basic food items that are ideal for long term storage, along with approximately how long they'll last for once stored.

If stored properly, these particular items can last you almost indefinitely.

White Sugar

Alcohol

Salt

Brown Sugar

Raw Honey

Hard Grains: If stored correctly, will last around 10 to 12 years.

Dry Corn

Hard Red Wheat

Buckwheat

Durum wheat

Kamut

Spelt

Soft White Wheat

Millet

Soft grains: If kept sealed will last around 7 to 8 years.

Quinoa

Barley

Oats

Rye

Beans: If kept sealed will last around 8 to 10 years.

Lentils

Lima Beans

Pinto Beans

Adzuki Beans

Kidney Beans

Black Turtle Beans

Garbanzo Beans

Flours, Mixes, and Pasta: If properly stored, will last around 5 to 8 years.

Pasta

White Flour

Coconut oil

Whole Wheat Flour

White Rice

All Purpose Flour

Cornmeal

Miscellaneous Items: If properly stored, will last around 2 to 5 years.

Canned Vegetables & Fruits

Canned Meats

Hard Candy

Canned Tuna

Tea

Peanut Butter

Dried herbs and spices

Coffee

Powdered milk

Fruits and vegetables that can be properly stored for at least 2 months or more.

Carrots

Sweet potato

Pear

Apples

Rutabaga

Garlic

Dry beans

Turnip

Cabbage

Onion

Beet

Grain corn

Celeriac

Parsnip

Leek

Pumpkin

Shallot

Celery

Potato

Winter Squash

As can be seen from above there are a lot of different foods you can begin storing now for future use. It's important to have a fully stocked food bank when prepping for a disaster, or when trying to live off the grid. Not only will these items allow you to still enjoy many of the foods you love for years to come, but you never know when you'll have a bad winter or an issue with your animals producing food. It's good to have reserves in case something doesn't go according to plan.

Remember to have all your storage systems in place before prepping in earnest. This will save you a lot of time and energy. If your systems are not in place it will be harder to track what you have, what you need, and when things are set to expire. I label everything that goes into my storage with the name of the item, the amount, the date it entered storage and the date it's set to expire. I then also enter these things into the ledger I keep and it allows me to have all the information I need on hand and easily accessible. I also always rotate my food putting the items with the longest expiration dates in the back and moving up the soon to expire stuff so I know to use it before it goes bad.

A Guide to Water Storage

Water is without a doubt the most important thing a human being needs for continued survival. You need a certain amount of water every day or your odds of surviving through an SHTF situation starts to plummet dramatically. Water is used not only for quenching our thirst, but it's also crucial in the preparation and growing of food, washing, and cleaning.

Any proper SHTF stockpile will have a heavy emphasis on water storage, and a detailed plan for how to go about replenishing it once the supply has begun to run low. You need to be in a location with not only a reliable and clean water source but a water source that is also plentiful and secure. You should focus some of your time on really learning as much as possible about finding new water sources, and ways to properly filter your water.

A solid rule when you're stockpiling is that every person in your group will approximately use one gallon of water every day. Using this approximation will allow you to roughly estimate how long your water will last, and at what point you need to replenish your supply. Once you've gone through your supply a few times, you can adjust your time frames depending on how much actual water you and your family uses.

Also, it's a good idea to have a few different water sources in the event one ever gets contaminated. You also want to make sure your bug out locations are all near water and meet the criteria above. This will give you plenty of options, and ways to pivot depending on what the situation dictates. Another good idea is to always carry water with you when venturing out in case you get stuck somewhere or delayed from returning home.

Personally, I invested in good rainwater collector along with a top of the line filter. This allows me to use filtered rain water when doing chores like washing my clothes or bathing. There's no reason to tax my drinking supply of water when it isn't necessary.

I suggest having at least 150 gallons of long term water storage if you have the room for it. I doubled this and have 300 gallons of water storage. I have my water stored in a big 50 gallon drums stacked vertically. I could have stacked them three high but I had extra room so I stacked them two high in three spots right next to one another. It made it a little easier that way for me to refill them when necessary. Feel free to use whatever setup you like, everyone I know has a different way of doing things. The important thing is you have the storage in place.

Chapter Three: A Guide to Bugging Out and Creating The Perfect Bug Out Bag

Creating The Perfect Bug Out Bag

In this section, I'm going to go over what items you'll want to have in order to create the perfect bug out bag. Remember, every member of your group needs to have their own bug out bag. I stock all of my bags exactly the same, except for the clothing, which contains the same items just in the different appropriate sizes.

The first thing you need to decide on is the bag itself. There are many great options out there but I personally use an Osprey Atmos 65 backpack. This allows me the room I need for my items plus it doesn't add a lot of extra cargo weight. With everything packed, including my tent, it weighs approximately 30lbs. This weight doesn't account for any food and water I may be bringing with me. You'll need to add a few more pounds for that. I suggest doing a little research and seeing what kind of options are important for your needs. I went through a few bags before finally settling on this one.

I did make some adjustments to my bag like taking out all the internal bags and switching over to ultralight bags to cut down on weight. I also use packing cubes to help organize my items and cut down on the space they take up in my bag. These work wonders for staying better organized and I suggest you look into purchasing some.

I have my gear set up and organized into different bags. I use a survival tools bag, medical bag, clothing bag, toiletries bag, electronics bag, tent bag, sleeping bag, and my cooking set. Having these things separated and labeled cuts down on the time I need to find what I need.

Before packing, I also lay everything out and double check my list to make sure I haven't forgotten anything. Don't skip this step! You don't want to be in a situation where something you need isn't available because you were too lazy to double check your bag.

Here I'll break down each of the bags and what items I keep in each one. Remember, everyone's situation is different, so feel free to add or subtract anything as you see fit. There is no one bug out bag that will work for everyone. Take into account your location, your budget, and your skills when finalizing what you'll add to your bag.

Tent Bag / Sleeping Bag

Choose whichever brands you want. Just make sure they are durable, lightweight, waterproof and fit any size requirements you may have. I always carry a tent, sleeping bag, tarp, ground pad and a wool blanket in each of my bags.

Survival Tools Bag

In this bag, I keep all the tools I'll need to help me survive. Here is the list of items I keep in my personal bag:

Maps + Schedule of all Bug Out Locations and Rendezvous Points

Mini Filtration System & Straw

Folding Pocket Knife + Multi-Tool

Lighters (I always carry a few extra)

Candles + Matches +Fire Starter (I always have multiple options for starting fire)

Emergency Mylar Blanket + Fishing Kit + Snare Wire

Adjustable Wrench + Scissors + Tape Measure

Headlamp w/ Spare Battery + Flashlight + Red Slip On Filter (Night Vision)

Key Chain Light + Signal Mirror

Chainsaw w/ Extra Hand and a small container of Olive Oil

Hatchet + Binoculars + Sewing Kit

Pepper Spray + Duct Tape

Paracord / Rope Tightener / S Clips

Handgun + Ammo (These are part of my bag & my wife's bag only, not my kids)

Clothing Bag

Socks (4 Pairs)

Single Layer Polyester Long Sleeve Shirt

Dry Base Layer Pants

Fleece or Jacket

Underwear (4 Pairs)

Wool Hat

Waterproof Rain Gear (Poncho)

Boots (1 Pair)

Shoes (1 Pair)

Work Gloves

Shirts (3)

Pants (3)

Electronics Bag

Encrypted Thumb Drive (With Personal Information + Backup of Documents Binder)

Ham Radio + Charger

Phone + Charger

Laptop or Hand Held Tablet + Charger

Batteries (All Sizes Needed)

Crank Power Charger

Medical Bag

Bandages (Different Sizes)

Tourniquet

Neosporin

Combat Gauze (Quick Clotting)

Sunscreen

Moleskin

Compress

Advil / Tylenol

Any Prescription Medications

Toiletries Bag

Liquid Soap

Aloe Vera

Antacid

Toothpaste / Toothbrushes

Hand Sanitizer + Wet Napkins

Chapstick (2)

Dental Floss

Ear Plugs

Gold Bond Body Powder

Shampoo

Toilet Paper

Cooking Set

Wood Burning Backpacking Stove

Trangia Alcohol Stove w/ Yellow Heet (Alcohol Stove Fuel)

Titanium Pot w/ Frying Pan Lid Combo

Metal Plate + Metal Cup

Lightweight Folding Spatula

Seasoning (Salt / Pepper)

Sugar

Can Opener

Spork

MRE"s

Water Purification Tablets

Pot Scrubber

Pot Holder

Water & Food

The last step of any good bug out bag is having the proper amount of food and water rations. Water is essential and you need to have a bare minimum of 1 liter for every day you think you'll be on the road. I always err on the side of caution and bring a few extra liters more than I think I'll need. I 'd rather the extra weight than not having water when needed.

When it comes to food you want to have at least 3-4 days worth in your bag. I like to keep protein bars and MREs as my main bug out bag food items. You can add whatever you'd like but these are what I personally back my bags with. I normally carry 8 protein bars and 5 MREs in my bag. I find this is good for 4 days, or even 5 days if I need to stretch it out another day.

A Brief Guide to Bugging Out

At some point, you might be faced with the difficult decision of either bugging in at home or bugging out to a different location. If you've prepared properly for every scenario you're chances of success will be much higher. In this section, I'll go over my personal strategy for bugging out.

First off, if at all possible you should have a destination planned out with supplies already stored there in case of an SHTF situation. If the world begins to collapse around you, make sure you know multiple evacuation routes out of your city or town. Not preparing a bug out location in advance means you haven't done enough preparation and could leave you in a dangerous position if you're not able to locate a safe area that can meet your needs quickly.

A great acronym I've seen used before to describe the steps you need to cover when bugging out is "LAST OUT".

L for location.

A for alternative routes.

S for supplies.

T for timing.

O for Observation

U for uniformity

T for transportation

Let's break down each of these steps a little further.

Location

In a perfect situation, you and your family will all be together, and able to communicate when disaster strikes. More often, that doesn't end up being the case. That's why it's very important that everyone who is part of your group knows not only the rendezvous location to meet at, but also where the end location is, and where the bug out bags are located. If you're able to afford it you may also want to invest in small HAM hand radios to better communicate with one another if ever separated.

Alternative Routes

It's very important that you have at least two different routes mapped out with different rendezvous points along the way to the end location. Your first route should be the best option if roads are open and there hasn't been mass panic. You should still avoid major cities but you can travel through smaller towns.

The second route will detail not only how to reach your end location avoiding all major cities, but also all smaller towns, especially any that use tunnels or bridges and cross some key terrain like gorges, mountains, or water. This can be a daunting route to plan depending on your location, but it's important to do it, even if it takes a lot of work to plan.

Rendezvous points are important. You needed to set a few of these along the way in case you ever get split up or need to pivot to a new location because an area was compromised. You should be able to adjust your route from every rendezvous point so you can still reach your final location.

I keep schedules and maps sealed in tubes in every vehicle my family owns, along with a copy in each bug-out bag. These maps are incredibly important and are treated as such. I've also made it a point to practice the route with everyone on multiple occasions. It's easier to learn by doing it, rather than by following a map with no real frame of reference.

Supplies

I keep my bug out bags around 30lbs each. This way there able to hold everything we might need during our travel but light enough where it won't hinder our progress too much. I went over everything included in my bug out bag during the last section.

Timing

Timing is a crucial element to our chances of survival, that is often overlooked. Once you think the writing is on the wall and your area will be compromised, it's time to head out to your bug out location. Waiting too long can lead to you getting killed, injured, trapped, or separated from your loved ones. It's better to leave early and be wrong than to leave too late. If you're wrong you can always just chock your bug out mission as a dry run, and return to your everyday life with a little more experience.

Observation and Intel

Practice observing your surroundings. Get good at noticing patterns and gathering intelligence. If the time ever comes, having those skills will come in handy while on the road. It will allow you to make better and faster decisions when it comes to advancing on your route and avoiding possible pitfalls along the way. Practicing these skills will also allow you to get a better sense of when an emergency situation may be approaching, giving you a much-needed head start out to your bug out location.

Uniformity

If you're traveling with a group, having a uniformity of preps can be a key factor in your continued survival. You want everyone to have access to the same key set of items you'll need in order to survive. If everyone is prepped in their own way, this can lead to holes in certain areas that one person may have overlooked, leading to disorganization and other negative consequences.

Transportation

What are your planned modes of transport? In most bug out situations, you probably won't get far in a ground vehicle like a car or truck due to congestion on the roads, destroyed or raised bridges, and other hazards.

Motorcycles are a better option, but won't work well if you're traveling with family. Especially since there's nowhere to hold either your gear or extra gas. You can try to modify a bike by adding saddlebags to the side, and some other storage features.

Boats are a good option if you have one and plan on going to a location accessible by water. You need to make sure you have fuel and extra parts in case you break down on the water.

If you own your own helicopter or plane that would be a great option but not really practical for most people.

Most people ending up taking their vehicle as far as they can, and then going the rest of the way by foot. While it's the longest and most difficult way to travel it also allows for a lot of flexibility, and gives you the ability to avoid detection when needed.

A Brief Guide to Bugging In

In this section, I'm going to discuss what you need to do in order to properly bug in during an SHTF situation. This has advantages and disadvantages to bugging out. Here I'll discuss the steps you'll want to consider taking in order to prepare.

First, take inventory of all your supplies both food and otherwise. You need to know exactly what you have in order to properly put together a list of things you need to stockpile more of, and items you're good on.

Next, you'll want to take inventory of all your home defenses. Your home will be acting as a safe zone from the chaos outside. Therefore, you need to make sure it is up to the task before a crisis happens. Being at home gives you an advantage in that you'll know all the strengths and weaknesses of your home along with the surrounding area.

Having a good home security systems with cameras mounted outside will allow you to keep track of what's going on outside your home without exposing you to any type of attack or detection. I also suggest getting motion detectors that will turn on outdoor flood lights, so you can illuminate any people trying to stalk around your property.

Install deadbolts on every door. If you can afford it get stronger doors that can withstand a frontal assault. Your doors should be made of steel and free of any glass. You'll also want a peephole as an additional minor security measure. I also suggest having locking security grates over all your windows that can be unlocked from the inside, in case you ever need to escape.

Outside your home, you want minimum landscaping to avoid giving intruders any type of cover. I also have preps in place so I can cover my windows so no light can be seen from outside the windows.

You'll also want to have some weapons stored safely in your residence in case the need every arises. I have a small arsenal of guns, knives, and ammunition in case of an emergency. I also keep bear spray in each room so if someone gets in and catches me off guard I can reach that spray and try and blind my attacker.

You'll also want to have an escape plan in place. This leads into your bug out plan above. Always be prepared for every situation. The less thinking you need to do and the more action you can immediately be taking the better.

Chapter Four: The Art of Off Grid Living

An Introduction to Off Grid Living

Voluntarily choosing to live off the grid isn't for everyone. Some hardcore preppers think it will make them better prepared should shit hit the fan. While I agree on that point, I think simply being prepared for having to live off the grid is more than suitable for most preppers.

If you don't want to cut all ties to modern society and live without running water, electricity, television, Internet and phone service you don't have to. Just take the time to set up systems and purchase items you may need should you one day be forced to go off the grid. The more groundwork you lay in advance, the smoother the transition will be if you're ever in a situation where the grid goes down for an extended period of time.

The most important thing, in my opinion, is to have the right piece of land. If you're going off the grid you need to generate your own power and have an easy to access water supply. You'll also probably want some privacy and additional space to set up your different processes like a garden, solar panels, wind turbines etc. You'll also want a location that gets good sunlight and moderate wind. You want to also consider the distance away from hospitals and schools (especially if you have children).

Living off the grid can be expensive. You need a good amount of money to get started. Besides finding land and having an appropriate shelter, you may need to pay for a new septic system, solar panels or wind turbines, tools, supplies and materials for your projects, livestock and a host of other things along the way. Don't jump into this until you've gone over the financial aspects, and see what you can and can't afford.

Here is a list of items you may want to research further or add to your stockpile:

Solar Oven or Wood Burning Stove

Solar Panels / Wind Turbines / Battery Powered Generator

Solar Still / Composting Toilet / Water Filtering System

Trailer / Wood Cart

How to Survive When Disconnected From The Grid

So you've decided to cut the cord and become more self-reliant. This is a major step for any prepper. Once you've cut off your reliance to the grid you're making a big statement saying you're going to be self-sufficient and plan on surviving with only your mind, hard work, and ingenuity.

Before actually disconnecting from the grid, be sure you have all your plans in place. You need to determine how you plan on creating your own power. Do you want to use solar panels, battery powered generators, wind turbines? Maybe you plan on foregoing electricity altogether. I'm not quite that extreme, although I do have a combination of solar power and wind turbines with a generator as backup.

Besides electricity, you'll also want to figure out your septic and water systems. Do you plan on having a septic system and running water, or do you want to use an outhouse and collect / distill your own water daily from a local water source?

How about your refrigerator and other appliances? Do you plan on using propane for your heating and powering appliances? Maybe, you'd rather use a solar oven or wood stove to cook all your food. Do you want to heat your house with a solar furnace or wood burning fireplace? There are no wrong decisions! Just be sure to be prepared and have the items you need all set in place before you go and turn off the power.

The worst thing you can do for your family is disconnect from the grid without being properly prepared. Once you are off the grid and all the processes have been put in place you'll have a big leg up over most people should a disaster ever occur. If the grid ever goes down you'll already be well prepared and set up for your future survival.

Personally, I still live primarily on the grid when at home. I have cut back on many of my costs by using solar panels to power some of my electronics. However I really don't want to live without the luxury of Internet access, television, and phone service unless I'm forced to.. My prepping plan focuses more on the aspect of growing my own food, stockpiling, using fewer resources, and preparing my home in case some type of crisis every does occur. I have a solar oven and some other off the grid items stored away with my supplies so if the day ever does come I can make the switch to off grid living much less painful.

Chapter Five: 20 Skills You'll Want to Learn and Master to Survive

20 Skills You'll Want to Learn and Master to Survive

Having both a plan and a stockpile is simply not enough to survive long term during a disaster. You'll also need to have survival skills and specialized training. This chapter will go over 20 skills you'll want to know in order to increase your odds of survival. Practice and learn these skills now, so if the time ever comes you and your loved ones will be prepared for whatever obstacles are thrown in your direction.

1. Learn Some First Aid – At the very least you need to have a well-stocked first aid kit and a few manuals on what to do in certain life medical situations. I also suggest taking some first aid classes. Learn how to perform CPR, and also how to bandage and treat wounds properly. The more medical skills you have, the better your long-term odds of staying alive.

2. Learn How to Properly Find and Hunt Your Own Food - Learning how to properly hunt and gather your own food is vital to your family's chance at survival. Learn what types of plants are edible, and what kinds are inedible. Learn what kinds of animals live in your region, and the best ways to trap and hunt them. You'll also want to learn how to fish and set crab traps.

3. Learn to Locate and Purify Water – This is a skill you have to learn. Even our best-laid plans can come undone in a moment. If you're ever forced away from your primary water source, you'll need to learn how to quickly find new ones, and also how to go about purifying the water you do find so that it's clean enough for you to drink.

4. Learn to Sew and Repair Your Clothing – These skills are great to know and will come in handy very often. Take the time to learn how to sew, how to repair any torn clothes, and even make some new clothes if necessary.

5. Learn to Start a Fire and Keep It Going – You need to multiple ways to get a fire going quickly with or without any of your stockpiled fire starting tools. It's also important to know how to keep your fire going once it's gotten started.

6. Learn Weapons Training and Self Defense – Train yourself and your family in the ways of self-defense. You also want everyone in your family to learn how to safely use and properly maintain a weapon.

7. Learn to Train Your Mind – You need to have the right frame of mind and a strong will in order to successfully survive a disaster long term. I often practice mental exercises to help keep my mind sharp and focused in the event there 's an emergency one day.

8. Learn Hygiene and Good Grooming Skills – Keeping yourself groomed and clean will go a long way in helping to fight off any types of bacterial infection and diseases. Without modern medicine getting sick can turn deadly fast so preventing any illnesses is very important.

9. Learn How to Build a Shelter - Learning to take the items around you and turning them into a secure and dry shelter could be the difference between your life and death.

10. Learning Navigation – When traveling if you ever need to deviate from your plan knowing how to navigate is what will save you. This skill is also very useful for scouting trips and hunting trips. The last thing you want to do is get lost in the woods.

11. Learn to Cook From Scratch – In an SHTF situation, there won't be a grocery store you can get your food from. Knowing how to cure your own meat, make your own cheese, bread, and alcohol is a big key to thriving off the grid. You should also learn how to dehydrate and preserve your food for long term storage. I suggest taking a few culinary classes.

12. Learn to Garden - Having a green thumb is critical if you want to survive long term after a disaster. Growing your own food will provide the backbone of your diet going forward. If you're not able to replenish your food eventually you'll run out and starve.

13. Learn to Compost – This skill made a tremendous difference in both the quality and the amount of food I was able to grow in my garden.

14. Learn Backyard Beekeeping – Bees are a great source of honey. The great thing about honey is it can last almost indefinitely making it a wonderful item for long term food storage. The beeswax is also great for making candles and a variety of other items.

15. Learn to Raise, Breed, and Butcher Livestock – If you're able to have your own livestock you'll be in an enviable position after an SHTF situation. Animals are great sources of food and materials like wool. Knowing how to properly raise these animals, breed them and eventually butcher them will go a long way in ensuring your family stays well fed.

16. Learn Animal First Aid – If your animals are a big part of your long term food supply, knowing how to take care of them and prevent illness is a big deal. One outbreak untreated can wipe out all your animals.

17. Learn Carpentry and Other Building Skills – When on your own you're responsible for building and fixing everything. You'll want to learn as many skills as possible. The handier you are the easier life off the grid will be.

18. Learn to Be Your Own Mechanic - Knowing how to properly change your oil, your tires, and fixing other common problems with your vehicles is a valuable skill to have. You don't want to be stranded in case you ever need to bug out quickly.

19. Learn to Defend Your Home – You need to protect your property from intruders. Learn how to set warning signals and traps around your property, while also learning how to make your home itself safer and more secure.

20. Learn to Think Outside The Box – Creative solutions to problems will be needed when living off the grid in an SHTF situation. Knowing how to come up with workable solutions on the fly is an important skill to learn for your continued survival.

Chapter Six: 100 Tips & Tricks on How to Prepare Your Family For Disaster

100 Tips & Tricks on How to Prepare Your Family For Disaster

By now you've made you survival plan and created your stockpile list. Here are 100 tips and tricks on how to get prepared in case of an SHTF situation.

1. Install security around your property. Secure your doors and windows. Add strike plates to your exterior doors and add some barbed wire around your perimeter.

2. Have vehicles stored safely where you can access them quickly.

3. Have a bug out plan in place with multiple exit routes planned. Have an easy way to access your bug out bags in case you need to leave quickly.

4. Have more than one location you can go to in case a certain area gets compromised, and you can no longer reach it. I suggest having stockpiles started in each of those locations.

5. Learn all the survival skills I discussed in the last chapter. Knowledge is power when you only have yourself to rely on.

6. Practice your first aid skills. The more you use them the more they'll become like second nature.

7. Practice using your weapons. Run safety drills, and go the firing range to constantly hone your skills.

8. Hold emergency drills. Being calm in an emergency can mean the difference between surviving and not surviving. The best way to stay calm is to know your exit strategies down cold. Drilling monthly will allow you to know what works, what doesn't, and will also get you used to bugging out in a hurry. I hold drills at different times of the day and night to keep my family off balance. You want your drills to feel realistic.

9. Keep your plans private. Don't loop in a lot of people about your prepping plans. Those same people may come and try and steal your preps in an emergency situation. Don't give anyone but your group your SHTF stockpile location or your final bug-out locations.

10. Always keep prepping. Your work is never done. There is always a better, more efficient way to do things. Not only that, but you'll need to rotate in new preps occasionally before old preps expire.

11. Use crayons as an emergency candle.

12. You can use toilet paper and duct tape to make a splint that will help set broken bones.

13. You can help fight off frostbite by applying baby oil to your skin.

14. Save all your empty water bottles for extra water storage. Especially good if you need to travel, and need smaller containers to hold water in.

15. Start building your prepper library now. It's a good idea to try and stock up on DIY books and how to guides. If you don't know how to do something these books can walk you through the problem and give you some needed answers.

16. Start connecting with other preppers in your area and build a community. It's easier to do things when you have like-minded people who can help.

17. Start exchanging some of your money each month for precious metals. If society collapses paper money will have no value but people will still barter with silver, gold, diamonds, food and supplies.

18. Make a safe place to store ice. This will allow you to store meat and other perishables for a longer period during the winter months without worrying about animals getting into it.

19. Keep your generator in a safe and well-guarded area. These are hard to conceal when running, and will be the target of thieves in your region. Only run the generator when necessary so as not to draw too much-unwanted attention.

20. Storing seeds are great, but crops can fail so don't only store seeds. Make sure you have a full preppers pantry just in case you're garden takes some extra time to get going.

21. If you're bug out plan involves a lot of walking. You need to start getting into shape now. Walking for long distances with a 30lb+ bug out bag on your back is a recipe for over exertion and possibly worse. To live off the grid you need to be in very good physical condition. It's hard work doing everything yourself!

22. Start storing firewood now! You need a large source of dry firewood to keep your home heated and fire going long term. Having a large supply of firewood on hand will make life a little less stressful. You also want to have a dry area to store your wood.

23. Perform regular maintenance on your home, vehicles and weapons. No one knows when a disaster will strike, so make sure to stay on top of any issues with your most important assets. The last thing you want is to let things fall into disrepair right before SHTF.

24. Baking soda and baking powder work for a ton of things. Use them to eliminate odors, remove stains and to scrub your countertops and sinks with.

25. You can use 5-gallon buckets to easily make a chicken water and feeder.

26. You can mix apple cider with your animals food or water to help boost their immunity.

27. Use some black plastic sheeting in order to warm up an area of soil for some planting.

28. You can poke holes in the lids of gallon jugs and use them as watering cans.

29. Learn how to install your fence without having to dig into the ground. Especially useful in rocky areas or in areas with large root systems.

30. Freeze your eggs to keep them from going rotten.

31. You can use duct tape to help you open jars easily.

32. You can use parts from an old bike to make a crossbow.

33. Save your coffee grounds. They can be used in your compost, they can be used as plant food, they can be used in cooking, and they can be used to deodorize your hands or fridge after dealing with smellier items like onions or fish.

34. 2 Liter soda bottles are great for storing rice and beans in.

35. You can use lightweight branches and a tarp to make a raft.

36. You can create a makeshift candle out of a jar of Crisco.

37. Chips like Doritos can make great tinder if you need to start a fire in a pinch.

38. You can cut holes in garbage bags to make a quick rain jacket.

39. You can use your eyeglasses to magnify the sun and start a fire with your tinder.

40. Don't store water in old milk jugs. It's hard to clean out all the milk residue and that can lead to dangerous bacteria beginning to form in your water.

41. Have multiple caches for your preps. If you store all your preps in one place and it gets compromised you'll have nothing to fall back on.

42. Don't forget about prepping for your pets. Many people accidentally overlook this one.

43. Always test everything yourself. That goes for all your weapons stockpile, as well as any tools or other items you have stored. You don't want to run into a situation where something is broken at the time it's most needed.

44. Buy a few bicycles and small trailers you can attach to them. This will make it easy to get some supplies moved around your property or back and forth from neighbors.

45. Know your local and state laws. In my town, there's an ordinance against storing more than 2 cords of firewood. While you want to get prepared you don't want to get fined or in trouble with the law while doing it.

46. If your Zippo lighter runs out of fuel you can still make a fire using it. Take the cotton inside the lighter, use its flint to create a spark and help ignite the cotton.

47. Always carry some aluminum foil on you. It is great for laying on the wet ground in order to make a dry platform to help build a fire.

48. Put masking tape on your flashlight lens to reduce your profile to others but still have enough light to get your task completed.

49. Learn to navigate at night by using just the stars. Just by learning a few constellations you can easily figure out the direction you're headed in.

50. If you're not able to afford a stab resistant vest you can use a homemade vest with carbon steel saws. Just combine a bunch of saws using duct tape in order to create a stab proof plate you can put in a vest for added protection.

51. Bleach can purify your water. The needed ratio is 2 drops of unscented bleach to purify one liter of water.

52. You can use toothpaste in order to treat insect stings and bug bites.

53. You can lay tent pegs across two logs and turn it into a makeshift grill.

54. You can use just a thorn, a can, and a little bit of string as a fishing kit when you're in a bind.

55. If you're in wet conditions you can easily get tinder by shaving off some strips from the bark of logs and twigs.

56. Place large rocks around a fire to help absorb heat. Even when your fire begins to die down the rocks will still radiate heat to help keep you warm. You can also put the rocks in the water to help boil and purify your water.

57. You can add the unpleasant smell from some water by adding charcoal to the water while it's being boiled.

58. Duct tape a foil blanket inside of your tarp shelter when out in the woods to increase the heat in your shelter.

59. When away from your home carry glow sticks. They can be tied to some paracord and swung around to create a large disk of light in case stranded and need to be rescued by your group.

60. Disposable ponchos are great not only as rain coats but as temporary shelters, and can also be turned into a solar still to help you gather up and purify water.

61. Always keep some water purification tablets on you in case you can't start a fire to boil some water.

62. Don't every use untreated water to clean your wounds. Also don't run your hands through untreated water if you have grazes or cuts on them.

63. You can use animal entrails as bait for your snares, traps, and fishing trips.

64. Always process your game far away from your house as not to attract any unwanted predators to your doorstep.

65. If ever stung but some stinging nettles combat the acid injected by their needles by spitting on area right away and scrubbing it very hard with your clothing to help get the acid out and off you.

66. You don't need to waste your energy and time chopping every log with a machete or ax. Just kick them, and snap them using force. Unless it's for furniture they don't need to be perfect.

67. Always carry some form of cash with you in your bug out bag. For at least a short time cash will still be an accepted form of currency.

68. When making a temporary shelter be sure not to lay on the ground. It will suck the heat out of your body. Instead make a small platform out of sticks or logs and place your sleeping bag on top of that. It will help you retain needed body heat.

69. When you pack your bag always put your light equipment on the bottom and heavier stuff on the top in order to help maintain a good center of gravity.

70. If you're going to be doing a lot of physical activity wear less clothing. As long as you're in continuous motion and dry, you can drop all your layers and still be comfortable. You don't want to sweat in cold weather as this will make your clothes wet, and can lead to hypothermia.

71. Carry some cigarettes even if you're not a smoker. It can be helpful when around other people to help you make a new friend or calm someone down.

72. Smoke is also a natural repellent for insects. You can wave around your jacket and other gear in the smoke in order to help keep yourself from getting eaten alive by ants and mosquitoes.

73. Socks can make good filters for getting dirt and other crap out of water.

74. When you get a blister, use a needle, and thread it through your blister in order to drain it. The thread will keep the holes you made open, and help to soak up any other moisture. Then place duct tape over your blister to help eliminate friction and any new blisters from starting to form.

75. Don't drink a lot of water when on an empty stomach. It will disrupt your bodies electrolytes and can cause shock in extreme cases.

76. Always set up camp on elevated ground and away from water. Water draws more insects, and can lead to you getting eaten alive at night.

77. Avoid tobacco! Tobacco will decrease your stamina. It limits your blood and oxygen flow to the brain. It also slows down blood clotting and healing by destroying some of the platelets that are in your blood.

78. Just because you see an animal drinking from a source of water does not make it safe. Many animals can drink and eat things dangerous to humans.

79. Only drink the milk out of green coconuts. The milk out of older or even ripe coconuts contains more oil that can act as laxative. This can lead to dehydration from a bout of diarrhea.

80. If you ever lose your machete or knife you can make yourself a sharp edge by simply smashing together 2 rocks.

81. Learn to waterproof all your gear.

82. Learn how to communicate with your family or group using hand signals so you can communicate in silence if necessary.

83. Take bathes using rainwater. Don't waste your stored water on staying clean.

84. Always quickly dispose of your garbage. If you're not afraid of attracting attention you can burn it. Otherwise, you need to cart it to a new location. Letting your garbage pile up will attract pests and rodents.

85. Dip cotton balls into petroleum jelly and then store in small baggies. They can make great fire starters when out in nature.

86. Start a mini lumber yard. Stock up on lumber now so down the road when SHTF you'll have a supply of good wood to use on any projects you need to construct yourself.

87. Before finalizing your bug out bag do a dry run carrying it around your house. Time yourself to see how long you can go before needing to put it down. If you can't go very long then you need to lighten the load.

88. Keep a running count of your ammunition. You don't want to start running low before a SHTF situation.

89. Have some Walkie Talkies stored so you can communicate over short distances with your group. This will come in handy quite often.

90. If you live in a city and SHTF situation occurs you're best bet is to get out as quickly as possible. Surviving long term in a city is a dangerous proposition. You're best bet is to have your bug out location in a more rural area. You want to get out before all the exits get jammed up or closed off.

91. Begin to purge your unnecessary belongings. You need as much space as possible for preps and supplies. Start evaluating and cutting down on items that aren't necessary or add value to your household.

92. Designate a common contact. If you get split up during an emergency and can't find each other at your rally points or bug out location have a person you can leave word with on your location. This won't work in all situations but in cases of hurricanes or smaller disasters having a person out of the disaster area you can all contact will help you stay in touch with one another until order is restored.

93. In an emergency situation you can use superglue to help seal up any wounds you have.

94. When installing a peephole in your door be smart about where you place it. I suggest placing it by the side of the doors near the door knob that way you can keep your body behind the door in case the person outside has a gun.

95. Have a every day carry kit on you. This is a few items that can fit in your pockets like a pocket knife, multi-tool, cash, and a lighter. If you carry a bag you might want to also include a flashlight and a small portable radio.

96. When bugging out don't dress like a prepper. Dress casually so you don't attract as much attention. If people think you're a prepper it will make you a target for thieves.

97. When you're bugging out and are in doubt, keep moving. Don't stay somewhere if you're not feeling safe. Trust your instincts.

98. Make plans for different types of emergency situations. Each type of SHTF situation can require its own specialized plan and escape route. Take the time to create plans for as many major scenarios as you can think of. You don't want to do all this work prepping and have it be for nothing, due to lack of planning.

99. Figure out a good system for getting rid of your bathroom waste. You want to have a plan for this in place before you need it.

100. Find time to enjoy your life and your time with family. Living off grid is hard work, you need to enjoy your life in order to make everything you're going through worth it.

Chapter Seven: 77 Items You Need to Have In Your SHTF Stockpile Now!

Basics to Starting Your SHTF Stockpile

You've answered all of the questions above, learned some good tips and tricks, even created a bug out bag for you and your family. In this section, I'm going to discuss setting up your stockpile. This includes your water, food pantry, medical supplies, tools and weapons.

Here is a small list of some of the key items you'll need to help keep your stockpile both secure and free of any issues.

1. AC Unit - At least while you still have some power it would be smart to have one of these items. Days can get awfully hot without any air conditioning. Enjoy it while you still can.

2. Resealable Airtight Containers – Everything you prep should be stored so you can see what it is, and should also be marked clearly with the contents, expiration date, and date it went into your stockpile. Airtight containers keep your food protected by keeping out moisture and bacteria. These are cheap to purchase so I suggest stocking up on them.

3. Shelving – Keep your food off the ground and on shelving whenever possible. I use heavy duty shelving in my setup and lots of it. Makes organization much easier.

4. Food Grade Buckets – Another great way for keeping food safe and dry.

5. Cleaning Supplies – Moisture isn't your only issue. You also need to worry about crumbs and dirt which can lead to bugs, pests, and rodents infesting your stockpile. Always keep your area clean. Animals carry tons of different diseases. The last thing you want in an SHTF situation is to get sick.

6. Security – Keep your stockpile a secret so others can't get to it. Also, keep it locked up as another layer protection. Everyone in my family has a key and of course knows the location of all the stockpile caches.

Once you've gotten your SHTF stockpile setup configured to all your specific preferences it's time to get started stockpiling all your items. A question I get asked a lot is how much should someone actually stockpile. The answer I give is simple! Prep as much as your space you have allotted allows you to.

You can never be to prepared. The more storage and preps you have ready and on hand the better. More preps mean you'll be able to survive for a longer period before needing to replenish your stores. It will also give you more items you can use when bartering.

Be sure to revolve your stockpile around the foods and items you're family actually needs and use. Don't get only what you're told to in the books. Make your prepping plan tailored for your needs. For example, you'll want to have any medications you need, or if you have pets you'll want to stockpile items they'll need.

Here are some preparation basics you'll want to add to your stockpile. Besides food and water, these items will come in handy.

1. Dutch Oven / Portable Camping Stove – Great for cooking. Just be sure to also carry plenty of extra canisters for fuel.

2. Bic Lighters / Candles / Stick Lighters – Great for both adding light and starting fires.

3. Multivitamins – A good supply of vitamins will help to fill in the holes for any nutrients you might not be getting on your limited diet.

4. Utensils, Paper Plates, Napkins, Disposable Cups / Paper Towels - With a limited amount of water to use for cleaning these are good alternatives and can be purchased cheaply in bulk.

5. Hand Mill – I love whole grain. It can be stored for long periods of time and is full of nutrients. However, it does need to be milled before being used so that's where having a hand mill comes in handy. I suggest using a manual one since you might not have access to power.

6. Bags - Having both smaller trash bags and heavy duty bags will be very useful for keeping your home clean. I have a large stockpile of bags in all sizes.

7. Seeds – Having a good collection of seeds is essential for long-term survival. This will allow you to grow all sorts of different crops to feed your family far into the future.

8. Can Opener – You'll be dealing with a lot of canned food so having a manual can opener on hand is a no-brainer. I suggest having multiple backups in case one or more every break.

9. Aluminum Foil – Great for both keeping items fresh and using to cook food over an open fire.

10. Dish Pans – Works great for cooking and using as a wash basin to clean not only yourself but also your clothes.

77 Items You Need to Have In Your SHTF Stockpile Now!

No stockpile is ever perfect. However, here are a bunch of items every serious prepper should strongly consider adding to their current stockpile if they don't already have them stocked. Different families will have different needs and different wants, but most of these items will be among the first to get scooped up when an SHTF situation strikes. Get prepared now, so you don't miss out later.

1. Toilet Paper – This is an important one for me. Some people don't mind not having this, but it's one luxury I'd prefer not to live without.

2. Alcohol – Not only good for drinking, it's also great for cooking and disinfecting your wounds.

3. Pain Medication – Reducing soreness, fevers, and general pain is a good idea if you want to stay healthy and sane. I suggest stocking up on these items as they'll fly off the shelves quickly when a disaster strikes.

4. Soap – Staying clean, and keeping things disinfected is important. You don't want to fall ill in an SHTF scenario if you can avoid it. I stockpile both liquid soap and bar soap.

5. Weapons – You need to make sure your family is protected. Having some weapons will also come in handy for hunting for food if necessary.

6. Ammo – Your guns won't work without ammo. Be sure to stock up!

7. Scissors – Much more convenient than a knife in many situations. Really handy if you're going to make your own clothes down the road.

8. Bleach – I have a big stockpile of this. Great disinfectant to have on hand.

9. Building Materials – The more materials you have saved up the easier you'll be able to make repairs around your home. You'll also be able to work on new projects that could make your life a little easier. I have a good sized collection of lumber, nuts, screws and bolts.

10. Ax – Great for chopping firewood. You'll be glad you have a few of these stockpiled.

11. Blade Sharpener – You're blades are of little use if there dull.

12. Batteries – I keep a stockpile of all sizes imaginable.

13. Salt – Not only will it be used to add flavor to food, it can be used to cure your meat.

14. Sugar & Honey – Two wonderful food sources that can be stored for an almost indefinite amount of time.

15. Instant Coffee – If you're a coffee drinker you'll be happy you stocked up on this. Instant coffee will last almost indefinitely.

16. Feminine Products – Besides there main uses, there also good for dressing a wound.

17. Freeze Dried Food – Commonly called MREs. These are great because they last a long time, and can be stored easily until needed.

18. Canning Supplies – You'll want to stock up on these as they'll be quite useful.

19. Preppers Library – Start building your collection of DIY guides and how-to guides now. You'll want books covering a wide range of topics you might encounter after an SHTF situation. There won't be an Internet to Google things on so you'll need reference guides on hand.

20. Firewood – Have a large store of firewood chopped and stored in a dry place.

21. Charcoal – If you're low on firewood you'll want some charcoal to help cook your food with.

22. Canned Food - A main source of food besides your garden.

23 Water – Can't live without it!

24. Wheat, Rice, Beans, Flour – Some of your key staple foods. Having a good stockpile of all of these is a good idea.

25. Gardening Supplies and Tools – You'll need the proper tools to efficiently manage your garden like shovels, rakes, hoes etc.

26. Cooking Utensils and Tools - Will make cooking much easier.

27. Toothbrushes, Floss, Toothpaste & Mouthwash – It's important to have good dental hygiene. Tooth pain can make life miserable. I also keep a store of Ambesol.

28. Jerky – Great long last meat that you can make in a wide variety of different flavors. Awesome food for stockpiling.

29. Milk – Condensed and powdered milk are both good things to stockpile.

30. Fishing Supplies – Fishing is a smart way to supplement your food stores.

31. Lighters, Candles, Oil, Fuel, Fire Starters – Being able to make fire is of the utmost importance.

32. Flashlights, Lanterns, Torches, & Glow Sticks – You need ways to move around in the dark.

33. Bathroom Supplies – Having shampoo, towels, razors, Q-tips will make life more pleasant. Good hygiene can help ward off illness and bacteria.

34. Soda, Gatorade & Kool-Aid – Any non-water type of drinks. Everyone can use some variety.

35. Hunting Apparel, Body Armor & Camouflage – You want to be able to move around unseen whenever possible, You also want some extra protection in case ever attacked.

36. Camping Gear – This will make traveling easier. Especially during hunting trips, or if you're forced to bug out.

37. Rope, Stakes, Spikes, Tarps, & Plastic Rolls – Everything you need to build a temporary shelter if needed.

38. Clothespins, Lines & Hangers – Good for drying your clothes after washing. It's important to keep clothes dry to prevent bacteria and mold growth.

39. Wheelbarrows & Carts – Excellent for moving around heavier loads.

40. Outdoor & Winter Clothing – You need clothes for all seasons of the years and for all situations.

41. Shoes & Work Boots – I have a stockpile of both. Your feet need proper protection.

42. Gloves – Heavy duty gloves will save your hands when working long hours outdoors.

43. Bug out Bags & Backpacks – These are crucial for supply runs, hunting trips, hiking trips and bugging out.

44. Electrical Tape & Duct Tape – They have a ton of uses.

45. Buckets – I have all sizes and shapes stockpiled.

46. Generators, Solar Panels, & Wind Turbines – If you can create power than you're already a step ahead of everyone else. Just be careful how you use it. It can make you a target.

47. Motorcycles – Great for shorter trips. Easy to navigate, and cheaper to fill with gas.

48. Hand Pumps & Siphons – Great for getting water, gas, and oil out of different tanks.

49. Chainsaw - This is one tool that will make life much easier.

50. Tools – Having a good supply of hammers, wrenches, screwdrivers, vices etc. will make your chores around the house easier.

51. First Aid Kit – You want to put together a comprehensive medical kit.

52. Prescription Medication – If you're forced to take any prescription medication you'll want to have a supply on hand if things ever go wrong.

53. Games – You'll want to have some type of entertainment on hand for your down time. Books, magazine, board games, cards, and dice are all good things to have on hand.

54. Portable Toilets – If you lose running water having one of these could come in handy. You can also get a composting toilet or build an outhouse.

55. Propane Cylinders – This will among the first things to go. Stock up on propane.

56. Fire Extinguishers – Handy in case you accidentally start a fire. Without one, you can lose your home from one accident.

57. Mosquito Coils & Repellent – You want to avoid constantly getting eaten alive by bugs.

58. Rain Gear & Ponchos – Keeping dry is always a good idea. Especially in the colder months.

59. Snowmobile – If you live in an area with lots of snow one of these will be essential in the winter.

60. Personal Items – Having extra items you need on hand is a good idea. For example, if you wear glasses have a few backups stored. If you wear dentures have another set made and plenty of denture adhesive.

61. Livestock – If you plan on raising animals start small now and start learning how to raise and breed them.

62. Pet food & Animal feed – If you have pets or are raising livestock you'll need supplies for them also.

63. Cots & Inflatable Mattresses - You'll want spare bedding on hand. You'll never know when you'll eventually need it.

64. Window Insulation Kits – Keeping the heat in your house is very important during the winter months.

65. Mousetraps, Rat Poison & Ant Traps - You need to control any infestations before they get out of hand.

66. Bicycles – For getting around your area quickly and cheaply.

67. Sewing Supplies & Fabric – You'll need these to mend and make clothes.

68. Garbage Cans – Good for trash and as extra storage.

69. Writing Materials (Pens / Pencils) – Will give you other activities to do in your downtime, and also good for keeping your logs of supplies and tasks that need to be done.

70. Journals, Scrapbooks, Diaries & Calendars – So you can write down your thoughts, remember important occasions, keep food logs, and keep track of time.

71. Coleman Mantles - Good for longer term lighting.

72. Hard Cheeses (Encased In Some Wax) – The wax prevents the cheese from growing mold and bacteria. Can last for many years this way.

73. Protein Bars & Protein Drinks – Good sources of needed nutrients.

74. Dried Pasta – Another great food to stock up on.

74. Dried Fruits, Raisins & Fruit Strips – My family loves these so we stock up on these pretty heavily.

76. Jams & Jellies – Another great addition to the stockpile.

77. Humidifier - It will help reduce some of the moisture in the room you have your stockpile located in. Bacteria begins growing when moisture accumulates in a small area.

30 Things to Stockpile With a High Barter Value

As you might expect, some of the items below will overlap with the list of items above. However items on this list I keep a separate stockpile of, solely for the use of bartering with if needed. I keep this stockpile away from my main stockpile to keep it easier to see what I have on hand for trade. Remember, you should never barter with any items that you and your family really need. You may not be able to find an item again once it's gone.

1. Silver & Gold – Many people believe this will be the only remaining form of real currency if a SHTF strikes. I try to store as much as I responsibly can.

2. Cigarettes – I don't smoke myself, but people who need their nicotine will trade almost anything to get it. That makes this a valuable commodity.

3. Alcohol – Another common want that people don't want to go without.

4. Batteries – If you want to power a smaller handheld item you're gonna probably need some batteries. That makes these very valuable.

5. Ice- If you figure out a way to store and create ice you'll be in an excellent bartering position.

6. Power - Items like solar power kits will be very desirable once the grid goes down.

7. Canning Lids – Most people forget about this one making it valuable if you have a stockpile of them. They are an essential part of preserving food.

8. Water Filters – Clean water equals survival. Having filters will make life much easier.

9. Seeds - People will need to grow food. In order to do that they will need seeds. This makes them great for bartering.

10. Medicine – People will always fall ill. Medicine will fetch a real premium in a SHTF situation.

11. Candles – People want to live in the light not the dark. Candles allow them to light up their evenings with very little hassle.

12. Ammo – You can always use some more bullets for your guns.

13. Toilet Paper – Not something I'll trade away, which makes it all the more valuable to people who are like minded.

14. Camping Supplies - People will continually need sleeping bags, tents and other camping gear.

15. Detergent – Clean clothes is a luxury many people don't want to live without.

16. Battery Operated Radio – This will be a sought after item for people looking to get updates after a disaster strikes. People want to know what's going on.

17. Sugar, Salt & Honey – Three staples no one wants to go without.

18. Weapons – People will want to defend themselves. These can fetch a high premium.

19. Water – If you have extra that you're willing to part with, people will pay for not having to find it and filter it themselves.

20. Canned Food – People will always look to add to their food stockpiles.

21. Knowledge & Skills – If you were a handyman you can trade those skills in exchange for something you need. Will work with all types of things.

22. Fuel – People will always need more fuel to run their vehicles and generators.

23. Marijuana – People who have medical conditions will pay a great deal to get something to relieve their symptoms. Not my thing but a viable bartering item in a SHTF situation.

24. Milk & Cheese - If you've got a good source of fresh milk and cheese you'll get a premium for it.

25. Building Supplies - People will always need to do repairs and work on new projects. If you have extra supplies like screws, nails and lumber you'll be in a good position.

26. Vegetables – If you have a garden you can trade for lots of goods with your extra crops.

27. Tools – Having extra saws, hammers and ax's to trade with will fetch you a good price in return.

28. Entertainment – Items like books, board games and toys will be a popular item to trade especially among people with children.

29. Clothing and Sewing Supplies – If you can make your own clothes you can turn around and barter for things you're running low on.

30. Meat – If you breed your own livestock and have a surplus of meat you'll be a popular person to trade with.

Chapter Eight: Preparing Your SHTF Arsenal & Defending Your Home

Basic Guide to Gun Safety

People will purchase guns for varying reasons. Some people will purchase one for hunting, some for a target shooting hobby, and others will purchase for self-defense of their loved ones and property. When I finally bought my first gun the reason was as a way to protect my loved ones in the event of an SHTF emergency.

I learned pretty fast, that all the things I grew up learning about guns were mostly inaccurate. Television and movies are famous for how they depict weapons in a completely unsafe manner. Television and movies value looking cool, and over the top exaggerated action, to showing how a weapon should be safely handled.

When you own and operate a gun there are 4 strict rules that shouldn't be broken.

1. Don't point the muzzle of your gun at something, unless you're intending to shoot it.

2. Your gun is always loaded (even when it isn't, you have to treat it like it's loaded).

3. Don't place your finger on the trigger of your gun until you're ready to shoot it.

4. Always know what your target is, and always know what is beyond your target in case you miss.

Let's look at these four rules in more depth starting with the first one.

Don't point the muzzle of your gun at something, unless you're intending to shoot it.

Discipline is essential. At one point or another, almost all gun owners will have some type of accidental discharge. That's why not pointing your muzzle at something or someone can mean the difference between either life or death. For all you new gun owners your muzzle is the end of your gun barrel where your bullet gets fired out of. The other end, where you're bullet goes into your gun is referred to the breech.

Even if you've double checked your gun, and it isn't loaded, don't wave it around carelessly. You need to have good habits and doing things like this can lead to bad habits forming. Just forgetting to check your gun once and waving it around loaded can be enough to end up with someone getting seriously injured. Please always try and keep your muzzle in a safely pointed position.

Your gun is always loaded (even when it isn't, you have to treat it like it's loaded).

It's important to envision your gun as loaded all the time. If someone checks the gun right in front of you I still suggest personally checking to see if it's loaded. Discipline is important when handling weapons. If you take a lax attitude bad things can happen at inopportune times. Remember, you're responsible for no one getting accidentally injured with your weapon. If you always practice safely eventually it will become second nature.

One common mistake I often hear, is new gun owners forgetting to look if there's still a round loaded in the gun chamber. This can often lead to accidental discharges, and has been responsible for many accidental deaths. You need to learn how to properly check, not only if your gun is currently loaded, but you need to also know if it's unloaded.

Don't place your finger on the trigger of your gun until you're ready to shoot it.

Few things are as important as this. Don't ever have your finger simply resting on your trigger when you're not attempting to shoot. This will lead to an accidental discharge. I've often heard horror stories from people who didn't follow this rule and shot someone because they tripped or slipped while their finger was on the trigger.

I suggest keeping your trigger finger resting on the gun frame above your trigger guard. This will stop you from accidentally discharging. Remember, when you're in a high-pressure scenario, and the adrenaline is pumping you might accidentally squeeze the trigger when you hadn't meant to. Stress can make your body react in funny ways. Why take the chance when you don't have to.

Always know what your target is, and always know what is beyond your target in case you miss.

Bullets carry on for a long time after fired. If you miss your target you want to make sure there are no innocent bystanders who might get hit by a stray bullet. This is a mistake that can often be averted. You always need to know what you're shooting at before you squeeze the trigger.

10 Tips For Improving Your Self Defense Gun Skills

Owning a gun won't help you if you can't use it properly. Self-defense isn't target shooting. When in a life threatening situation you'll have seconds to act, and your stress and nerves will be at an all-time high. You need to train both your body and mind how to react to these types of scenarios. This section will go over 10 things you can do to help sharpen your gun skills.

1. Practice Often – Learn how to operate, clean and fire your gun. You want your weapon to feel like it's an extension of your arm. If you can react, and not think when in an emergency situation, you're odds of surviving improve dramatically. I suggest always taking classes with certified instructors. as well as special self-defense courses to give you an added edge.

2. Use Only Dummy Ammo – Practice both unloading and loading your weapon with multiple magazine and dummy ammo to help you get good at it. You can't be fumbling around to try and reload your weapon while you're life is in danger.

3. Always Keep An Eye On The Target – Many people make the mistake of looking downward when shooting and reloading. Practice always keeping an eye on the target when you're shooting, and when you're reloading.

4. Learn to Shoot Fast and Accurately – Being able to hit your target quickly might save your life. You need to be both fast and accurate when using your weapon. Time waits for no man, and if you're fast but inaccurate that's pretty worthless also.

5. Shoot With Both Your Hands – Learn to shoot with both dominant and non-dominant hands. You never know when a situation might dictate you shoot from a particular hand only.

6. Dry Fire Drills – This is good for saving money and time at the range. Here you're practicing with an unloaded gun. Be sure to go through all your safety protocols to ensure your weapon is unloaded. Then practice visualizing different targets from different positions and drawing your weapon from its holster.

7. Practice Firing On Moving Targets – If you're under attack you can't expect your attacker to stand still. Learning to shoot moving targets coming from you at all positions and angles will make you much better prepared for a real world scenario. I also suggest practicing from your knees, and while laying on your stomach.

8. Practice With A Holster – You need to be able to draw your weapon both quickly and cleanly from its holster. Not being able to do this means you're much less likely to escape unharmed.

9. Know How to Use Your Gun Safe – If someone breaks in your home you need to be able to reach your weapon quickly. Not being able to operate your gun safe correctly could put your family in grave danger. Personally, I run drills getting to my safe and opening it quickly. I've gotten so good I can open my safe blindfolded. Of course, I've been training for a few years now.

10. Find the Gun That's Right For You – I went through a few different guns before I found one I was really comfortable with. Everyone is different, so try a few different weapons at the range and find which one best suits you.

Preparing Your SHTF Arsenal

When putting together your SHTF arsenal remember you need more than just some good weapons. You also need plenty of ammunition, cleaning supplies to keep your weapons maintained, cases and safes to keep your weapons safely stored, and a bevy of spare parts in case something on your weapon wears down or gets damaged, and needs to be switched out.

People often remember the weapons and ammunition but forget the other items I mentioned. Now many people ask me what I think is the perfect SHTF weapon if you only had one weapon to choose. My response is that it's different for most people but personally I prefer a pistol, followed closely behind by my shotgun.

I chose the pistol because it's easier to keep on me and offers me more flexibility than the shotgun does. I have a few friends who feel the shotgun is the best weapon to have and another friend who hates guns but loves knives.

Here is my personal SHTF Arsenal and why I chose each weapon.

1. Pistol – My main weapon, and the one I carry most often. I have this primarily for self-defense and shooting small game when hunting.

2. Shotgun – Easy to use and cheap ammo make this a great weapon to have on hand in an SHTF situation. I also can use it for both defense and hunting.

3. Semi-Automatic Rifle – Great for hunting and shooting at longer distances.

4. Long Range and Small Game Rifle – I also have two additional rifles besides the semi. One is when I'm going for bigger game at longer ranges, and the other is for getting smaller critters.

5. Ammunition – I have over 2500 rounds stored for each of my weapons. I'm continually adding to my ammo because I feel it's also a great item for barter.

6. Cleaning supplies – I have everything needed to clean each of my weapons properly along with instructional books in case I ever need to make repairs.

7. Spare Parts – I also keep enough spare parts to complete two more of each of my guns (except my pistol). I have a few spare parts for that (need to stockpile more) and a second backup pistol.

8. Gun Safes, Cabinet & Cases – I keep all my larger weapons locked in a gun cabinet. I keep my pistols in two separate gun safes on different sides of my house. I always keep gun cases if I ever need to travel with my weapons (like the shooting range or in my RV).

9. Sprays – We have a stockpile of pepper spray and bear spray. You never know when it might come in handy.

10. Knives – I carry a smaller pocket knife on me at all times but whenever I go out in the woods I always carry a larger hunting knife.

11. Bow & Arrows – I have these stored although I still haven't gotten around to really getting good at using them yet.

12. Holsters – I have extra gun holsters for all my pistols stockpiled.

A Guide to Defending Your Home

Defending your family and home in an SHTF situation is life or death business. Depending on your location you can find yourself under varying amounts of duress from people either looking to harm you or steal your supplies and preps.

In this part, I'm going to discuss a few ways you can defend yourself and your home. Remember, always make sure what you're doing is allowed where you live. Many towns and cities have strict ordinances on what you can do on your property. Now I have all of these prepped and ready to go but some of the traps will only be implemented if a situation occurs and my family decides to bug in.

When defending your household you should try to accomplish a few different things. Having a plan thought out in advance will allow you the best shot at successfully being able to maintain your home defenses.

First off, I suggest trying to deter any intruders from the thought of even trying to trespass. You can install "trespassers will be shot on sight" and "beware of dogs" signs on your property. This often has a big psychological effect on would-be invaders because it shows you won't be an easy target.

Secondly, you need to have an alarm system set up to alert you of any threats. You can also install trips wires, motion detectors, barbed wire, and cameras to discourage trespassers.

Next, you want a few traps put into place to stop attackers before they get to your home. You can dig a few pits along your property with stakes in the bottom covered up by some light branches and twigs. Just remember where you placed them so you don't get injured.

If they do manage to reach your home, you'll want it to be secure. I suggest strengthening your home. By this I mean adding the best security door you can afford, along with deadbolts and door braces. You can also add removable bars to your windows or treat it with security film to make it extremely difficult to shatter.

Finally, if they make it into your home I would have some type of weapons you can access in each room. Good examples are pepper spray or bear spray. I also have a few other weapons stored safely in each room including my guns, taser, and knives. You should also know all your escape routes so you can get yourself and family to safety as quickly as possible.

I personally don't have these but I know many preppers who have bunkers underneath their homes along with escape routes to another point on their property from those bunkers. Feel free to prepare however much you feel is necessary.

Chapter Nine: 5 Functional DIY Prepper Project You Need to Try!

5 Functional DIY Prepper Project You Need to Try!

Here are a few projects to get you started. I suggest getting used to working on projects now. It will make you more prepared should an SHTF situation ever occur. Feel free to substitute in your own plans or designs. These are just some suggestions. The possibilities are endless.

DIY Project #1 - Building a Garden

Your long-term survival will depend on you growing food to feed your family. The easiest way to do this is by starting a garden.

There are numerous ways to build yourself a garden. The amount of space will determine the size of your garden, and how much food you can produce. Some people want large gardens with a variety of crops while others want smaller, easy to manage gardens with only a few staple crops. Some will want to go with a greenhouse while others will want their garden to remain outdoors. Choose the option that works best for you and your loved ones.

This project I'm sharing with you is one my friend found online and used to build their greenhouse. They've been happy with the result so I thought I'd include it. It will take a couple days to complete and will cost around $200 dollars.

Here is the link to the step by step instructions.

http://doorgarden.com/2008/10/27/50-dollar-hoop-house-green-house/#more-44

DIY Project #2 - Build Yourself A Triple Compost Bin

Having your own quality organic fertilizer is the best way to get the most production from your new garden. Creating a compost bin to make and store your own organic fertilizer is a good idea for anyone that's serious about starting a garden to grow their own food.

This DIY project is for a triple compost bin. It might take a couple of days to finish and your main cost will be the lumber used to build it.

Here is the link to the step by step instructions.

http://homesteadandprepper.com/diy-build-a-3-bay-compost-bin/

DIY Project #3 – Making a Fire

Being able to make a fire anywhere, and at any time is one of the most crucial skills you can have in your arsenal. This project will go over a few different ways you can create a fire starter to help you get a fire going with the least amount of effort.

Here's a link to a few easy DIY fire starter techniques.

http://www.survivopedia.com/diy-fire-starter-ideas/

DIY Project #4 – Building A Simple Rocket Stove

Rocket stoves are an amazing solution to cooking food when off the grid. Having an easy way to continue cooking outdoors is extremely important if you ever happen to find yourself in an SHTF situation. This DIY project is rather inexpensive to make, and it also won't end up taking too much of your time to get put together properly.

What's a rocket stove? It's a cooking tool that uses a very small amount of wood fuel (twigs & branches), that is lit on fire in a high-temperature combustion chamber. The heat formed during combustion produces a flame that will shoot up and cook any food placed on the cooking surface. Rocket stoves are a great tool for preppers to have since they are portable, easy to make, and fuel efficient.

Here is the link to the step by step instructions.

http://www.instructables.com/id/How-to-make-a-Rocket-Stove-from-a-10-Can-and-4-So/?ALLSTEPS

DIY Project #5 - Build Proper Water Storage

Water storage is paramount in an SHTF situation. If can't access clean running water you'll need to have a large amount of water properly stored in order to survive properly off the grid.

This project is one I personally used and continue to employ. It's not too expensive to make, and a friend and I were able to build it over a weekend.

Here is the link to the instructions:

http://www.instructables.com/id/Build-a-3-drum-rain-collection-system-better/

10 More Quick Helpful Project Ideas Every SHTF Prepper Should Consider

In this section I'll briefly give a few project ideas I think will help make great additions to your home once SHTF, and you're forced to live off the grid. Now all of these won't be needed by everyone. Everyone's living situation is unique. Some will have plenty of land, and some will have only a small area to work with. Differences in terrain, weather, population and personal needs will all come into play when deciding which projects to tackle.

1. Build storage for all your firewood. Firewood takes some time to properly dry and cure. You should always have a good supply on hand especially during the winter months.

2. Build a chicken coop. Raising and breeding chickens can be a great long-term source of food.

3. Build a vegetable garden that's self-watering. A wonderful way to continually grow your vegetables.

4. Build an outhouse. Great if you don't have running water, and don't want to buy a composting toilet.

5. Build a Honey Cow in order to keep bees for honey and wax production. Honey is a good food source and great to barter with.

6. Build some trash rocks to recycle any unrecyclable trash. A good way to turn trash into something pleasant to the eye. They can be used to make tables, benches, walls and other landscaping accents.

7. Build a Solar Food Dryer. Great way to dehydrate your food.

8. Build furniture. This is great for both personal uses and for trade.

9. Build tools and a wood cart. This will help make your chores and tasks around the house much easier to complete.

10. Build a water filter. Great for cleaning your water before you purify it.

Chapter Ten: A Brief Guide to Urban Prepping

A Brief Guide to Urban Prepping

Trying to survive a long term SHTF situation will require a lot of prepping, training and hard work. However, if you live in an urban area with a lot of people per square mile than you need to prepare yourself a little differently than someone who lives out in the suburbs or a more remote location.

The reasons for this are you'll most likely have less room to store your preps and to create projects for use down the line. Also, once a disaster does occur you'll most likely need to bug out.

I wouldn't suggest trying to make it long term in a city environment. You won't have space, privacy, or the ability to grow a larger garden. You'll also find it difficult to find access to clean water, and you won't be able to hunt for your own food.

Urban Prepping Tip #1 - Know all the routes out of the city you live in. Once SHTF, people will panic, and it will get rough out there real quick. It's a good idea to have your bug out bag ready, a bug out location scouted out, and knowledge of every viable route out of the city. A good way to get out quick is by using any old abandoned railroads, and following them out of town.

Urban Prepping Tip #2 - Once a blackout or power outage occurs, begin gathering all the water you can. Since you won't have easy access to water it's important to gather as much as you can before everyone else follows suit and does the same. If you've decided to bug in, be sure to fill up your bathtub, sinks, bottles, buckets and anything else you can with water.

Urban Prepping Tip #3 – Don't engage in fighting others. People will start to panic and get violent looking for supplies once a disaster occurs. Don't get drawn into anything unless absolutely necessary. You may get injured or worse which will greatly reduce you and your loved ones ability to survive long term.

Urban Prepping Tip #4 – Get creative when looking for food. If you're in the city and need to hunt for food don't forget to check vending machines, closed down gyms, an office building with cafeterias, and shut down restaurants.

Urban Prepping Tip #5 – Don't let your weapons or walkie talkies show when out in public. People will want to steal your preps and weapons, Showing that you have these items will make you a target.

Urban Prepping Tip #6 – Have an everyday carry kit (EDC) on you. This is a simple kit which will help you out in an urban disaster event. It consists of a Bic lighter, bottle of water, folding knife, some extra cash, multi-tool and a portable radio. You can fit these all nicely in a small laptop bag.

Urban Prepping Tip #7 – Go solar. Even when you live in a smaller apartment you can do a lot of things to reduce your need of power drawn from the grid.

Urban Prepping Tip #8 – When bugging out you may want to ditch your car or any other form of public transportation. Odds are the city will get completely gridlocked before you can get out safely. This could leave you surrounded by people looking to loot or riot. You want to avoid people as much as you can while bugging put.

Urban Prepping Tip #9 – Don't draw attention to yourself. Do not wear camouflage or give any indication that you've prepared for a disaster. This will make you a target. Jeans and a t-shirt will work just fine. You want to blend in, not stand out.

Urban Prepping Tip #10 – If you're bugging in don't go near your windows. You don't want anyone to know you're location. This is a safety measure I suggest following. Getting seen might make you and your home a target.

Urban Prepping Tip #11 – Have some environmental disaster gear stored in your bug out bags. This includes eye protection, respiratory / lung protection, hearing protection and hand protection.

As you can see there is a lot of things to consider when urban prepping. This is just the tip of the iceberg. If you plan on bugging in while living in an urban environment I suggest doing more research and making your home as efficient and prepared as possible for a long term SHTF situation.

Conclusion

Thanks again for purchasing my book. Hopefully, you've learned the importance of SHTF prepping and all benefits of being properly prepared and protected.

Learning how to rely on only yourself to survive is an amazing skill to have no matter what the situation is out in the world around you. The projects and lessons in this book aren't only good for protection, there also great for lowering your monthly bills and teaching you how to be one with nature and the environment around you.

I pray most of the things you've learned will never need to be used in an actual survival situation. While I can't predict the likelihood of an SHTF situation occurring, or in what form it will take, I know that by taking some time to train and prep I've but myself and my loved ones in the best position possible. As a parent, that's all you can really hope to do for the people you love.

Stay safe and I wish you the best of luck!

Made in the USA
Middletown, DE
14 September 2018